My shows only got bigger.

When I was eight, my mom moved us to a three-bedroom house that was right by an amusement park. That's right! A real amusement park!

I'd act out movies in our backyard.

My friends and little brother were the co-stars. If they weren't there, I'd pretend the chicken coop was my castle. Our chickens would be my loyal army.

By the time I was twelve, I realized there was real power in making people laugh.

The principal of my school—a man named Bernard Drake—realized it too.

He was the very first person to label my wild and fun behavior as . . .

I took his advice.

The next year, a friend and I put on our first amateur production, a play called *Charley's Aunt*.

It was the very first time I felt that wonderful feeling that comes from getting laughs on a real stage.

How much did I love it?

To have that starring role, I sold the tickets, swept up after, and even turned out the lights.

No matter what your dream is, if you want it, you have to work for it.

So that's what I did.

Was I a bit too enthusiastic? Sometimes.

When I was fifteen, during one musical, I did a dance with so much excitement, I fell into the orchestra pit and dislocated my arm.

When I was seventeen, my mom sent me to a fancy acting school in New York City.
It didn't go as I had planned.

The teachers made fun of how I spoke.
They said I had no talent: that I couldn't sing and couldn't dance.
All the other girls laughed at me.
They were tall and beautiful.
I was funny and . . . different.

Of the seventy students accepted to the school, they narrowed it down to twelve.

I didn't make it. I failed.

From there I tried being a dancer.

But nothing much changed.

I never let it stop me.

At one point, I was so poor, I was down to my last four cents.

That's it. Four pennies.

To eat, I'd wait for a customer to leave a restaurant, then I'd grab their leftover food before it got thrown away.

I went to so many tryouts, I even wore out my shoes.

But no matter how hard I tried, the message never seemed to change.

Eventually, I did find work. And then, with a bit of luck, I finally got my first big break in the movies.

I was twenty-one years old and selected to be one of the girls in the background of the movie *Roman Scandals*.

As the director came to inspect us all, I grabbed some red crepe paper, tore it into shreds, licked it and . . .

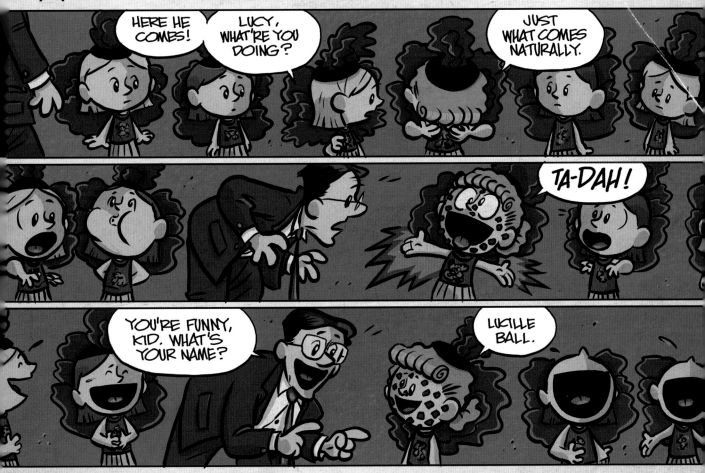

I stood out from the crowd that day.

From there, I got my first on-screen acting credit: in a short football comedy starring . . . the Three Stooges!

HEY, GUYS, WHAT'RE YOU—

NYUK NYUK NYUK

THIS GIRL'S FUNNY.

Most girls didn't want those slapstick parts.
I loved them. And I knew how to make them even funnier.

If you flinch when the pie hits you, the audience doesn't laugh as hard. I never flinched. It goes back to those days when my dad threw me in the air. I knew he was going to catch me. I knew I'd be safe.

In time, that confidence led to the one role that changed my life.
I had left movies and was working in radio.
Then CBS had a brand-new idea for a TV show . . .

To prove them wrong, my husband, Desi, and I took our show on the road.

We turned it into a vaudeville act.

Vaudeville was an old kind of show with lots of funny skits.

It became such a big hit, CBS decided it was ready for TV.
We asked for one thing: to film the show in front of a live audience.
Hearing that audience, people at home would really feel the laughter.

The TV network was worried about the cost of film.
They said it would be too expensive.
So we made a deal: They could pay us less money,
but the show would belong to us.

On September 8, 1951, the
bleachers filled up by 8 P.M.
I Love Lucy was ready to go.
And there was nothing "proper"
about it.

Every episode, Lucy and Ricky, along with their best friends, Ethel and Fred, would get into a crazy adventure.

IF ONE PIECE OF CANDY GETS PAST YOU, INTO THE PACKING ROOM UNWRAPPED, **YOU'RE FIRED!**

WRAP WRAP WRAP

ACK!

GULP!

GULP!

Every week, America tuned in to see what Lucy was up to. They wanted to see what new trouble I'd get into.

And they wanted to see who else would show up.

We had famous guest stars, like Harpo Marx and Superman. That's right! Superman!

Between 1952 and 1953, though the first TV bosses said no one would be interested, two out of three households with TV sets were watching *I Love Lucy* on Monday nights.

What was the secret of the show's success?

It was the thing I'd learned all those years ago.

You can always find a laugh in what everyone else is taking so seriously.

Today, people call me the greatest comedienne of my time and one of the most beloved entertainers ever. But I was also the first woman to run a major Hollywood studio.

Remember when I said the TV show belonged to us?
Our studio, Desilu, used the money from *I Love Lucy* to
produce other shows like *Star Trek* and *Mission: Impossible*.

In life, people put me down because I was different from everyone else.

They didn't like the way I looked, or the way I talked, or even the way I was always clowning around.

This isn't a joke: Don't let other people change you.

There's no such thing as a proper girl—or boy.

Be true to who *you* are.

Go look in the mirror.

When someone puts you down, *that's* who'll pick you back up.

When you get sad, *that's* who'll help you laugh it off.

To find happiness in life, you have to do what *you* do best.

Trust me on this: Every time you look in that mirror . . .

I am Lucille Ball.
I believe that humor can take on anything.

We all need laughter—every single one of us.
And for the best comedy, people have to believe in you.
But for that to happen, you have to believe in yourself.

Emmy Statuette
®TV Academy/
NATAS

I Love Lucy wasn't just the title of the show.
It was my most important life lesson:
In this world, the person you need to love most is *you*.

"*Love yourself first and everything falls into line.*"
—LUCILLE BALL

Timeline

AUGUST 6, 1911	1926	1928	1933	NOVEMBER 30, 1940
Born in Jamestown, New York	First amateur theater performance in *Charley's Aunt*	Moved to New York City to attend John Murray Anderson School for the Dramatic Arts	Made movie debut in *Roman Scandals*	Married Desi Arnaz

Lucy and Desi

A famous scene
from *I Love Lucy*

Lucy, age 2

JUNE 2, 1950

Vaudeville act
opened at the
Chicago Theatre

JULY 17, 1951

Birth of first child,
Lucie Desirée Arnaz

OCTOBER 15, 1951

First episode of *I Love
Lucy* aired on CBS

1952

Won first Emmy for
Best Comedienne

JANUARY 19, 1953

Birth of second child,
Desi Arnaz Jr.

APRIL 26, 1989

Died in Beverly Hills,
California

JULY 6, 1989

Posthumously
awarded Presidential
Medal of Freedom

Lila, this book is for you. It's also for
my Mom, your Nana.
She was full of personality, just like you.
She had the best sense of humor, just like you.
And when I was little, she used to show me all the
best TV shows so we could laugh together.
Lila, this is no joke: My love for you is endless.
—B.M.

For my favorite redhead, my mother-in-law, Phyllis.
She was always a proper lady but someone who
knew how to laugh.
I miss doing crossword puzzles and
watching the Mets with her.
Without her, there is just a little less
laughter in our world.
—C.E.

Special thanks to E.E., for going through so many of Lucille Ball's audio transcripts and for becoming
part of *our* family. This book wouldn't be the same without her.

. . . .

SOURCES
Desilu, too, LLC
Love, Lucy by Lucille Ball (Putnam, 1996)
I Love Lucy: Celebrating 50 Years of Love and Laughter by Elisabeth Edwards (Running Press, 2010)
Lucille Ball: Actress & Comedienne by DeAnn Herringshaw (Abdo Publishing, 2011)
Ball of Fire: The Tumultuous Life and Comic Art of Lucille Ball by Stefan Kanfer (Knopf, 2003)
"I Call on Lucy and Desi" from *The Saturday Evening Post*, May 31, 1958 by Pete Martin
Lucy—And I by Lucille Ball with Gladys Hall (unpublished manuscript from the Gladys Hall archives of the
Academy of Motion Picture Arts and Sciences)
Letter from Lucille Ball to Gladys Hall (from the Gladys Hall archives of the Academy of Motion Picture Arts and Sciences)

FURTHER READING FOR KIDS
lucy-desi.com: the website of the Lucy Desi Center for Comedy and the Lucy Desi Museum in Jamestown, NY

. . . .

DIAL BOOKS FOR YOUNG READERS
Published by the Penguin Group • Penguin Group (USA) LLC, 375 Hudson Street, New York, New York 10014

USA | Canada | UK | Ireland | Australia | New Zealand | India | South Africa | China
penguin.com

A PENGUIN RANDOM HOUSE COMPANY

Text copyright © 2015 by Forty-four Steps, Inc. • Illustrations copyright © 2015 by Christopher Eliopoulos

Library of Congress Cataloging-in-Publication Data
Meltzer, Brad.
I am Lucille Ball / Brad Meltzer ; illustrated by Christopher Eliopoulos. — pages cm. — (Ordinary people change the world) • ISBN 978-0-525-42855-8 (hardcover)
1. Ball, Lucille, 1911–1989—Juvenile literature. 2. Entertainers—United States—Biography—Juvenile literature. I. Eliopoulos, Christopher, illustrator. II. Title.
PN2287.B16M46 2015 791.4502'8092—dc23 [B] 2014035469

Manufactured in China on acid-free paper • 10 9 8 7 6 5 4 3 2 1
Designed by Jason Henry • Text set in Triplex • The artwork for this book was created digitally.